Tried and Tested Assessment Pa

GW01090725

Contents

Introduction

▼ This booklet contains eight assessments that allow teachers to determine easily the extent to which key mathematical skills have been mastered by Fourth Class pupils.

▼ Assessment can help the teacher and the child in a number of different ways. Firstly, it can show how the children are progressing in the different strands of the curriculum, providing a basis for future planning in those areas. Secondly, it can help in the pacing of work by indicating the strengths and weaknesses of a particular group, and lastly, it can play a diagnostic role in identifying particular areas of difficulty for a child.

Key Features

▼ Included among the new and exciting features are:

Third Class Skills

- A **Beginning of Year Assessment** that will quickly identify each pupil's strengths and weaknesses as they begin the Fourth Class programme, thereby facilitating early **planning and intervention** by the teacher. The Third Class skills are listed in the Maths Matters 4 Solutions Book.

Fourth Class Skills

- Five other assessments will enable the teacher to **track each pupil's progress** on an ongoing basis throughout the year.
- The **End of Year Assessment** on pages 20 – 25 will serve as a comprehensive guide to the overall progress of each pupil throughout the year.
- These six assessments are designed to test the pupil's **mastery of the 99 key skills**, which are outlined in the revised curriculum for Fourth Class. The Fourth Class skills are also listed in the **Maths Matters 4 Solutions Book**.
- Some of the **numeracy skills are retested**, reflecting the importance of giving pupils several opportunities to master those particular skills. For example, the problem-solving skills involving addition, subtraction, multiplication and division are tested in each of the six assessments.

▼ A multiplication and division facts assessment is provided on page 19. With the introduction of calculators in the Fourth Class programme it is important to measure the extent of each pupil's mastery of the basic multiplication and division facts.

▼ The Skills Record Sheets on pages 27 and 28 allow the teacher to indicate the skills mastered by ticking the appropriate box. For example, Box 1 on the Fourth Class Skills Record Sheet is ticked when the Fourth Class skill S1 is mastered. Skills not mastered can be indicated with an X.

Beginning of Year Assessment　　　Part One

1. Write the number shown on this abacus picture. **h t u**

   _____ S1

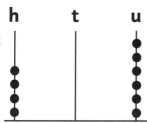

2. Write this number in digits. S2
   'Six hundred and eighty' _____

3. Write these numbers in order of size, beginning with the largest.
   289, 982, 398 _____, _____, _____ S3

4. Round 54 to the nearest 10. _____ S4

5. Round 861 to the nearest 100. _____ S5

6. 　245
   + 452
   _____ S6

7. 　469
   + 387
   _____ S7

8. 　587
   − 354
   _____ S8

9. 　651
   − 367
   _____ S9

10. There are 286 girls and 198 boys in St Peter's National School. How many children are there altogether in the school? _____ S10

11. When Shannon Harps were playing in the Cup Final last year, 620 supporters travelled to the match. 386 went by bus and the rest by car.
    How many travelled by car? _____ S11

12. Fill in the missing number: 6 + 6 + 6 + ___ = 4 x 6 S12

13. 6 x 9 = ___ S13

14. 9 x 0 = ___ S14

15. 4 x 8 = 8 x ___ S15

16. 7 x 5 = (___ x 5) + (4 x 5) S16

17. 　54
    x 7
    _____ S17

18. Martha bought 5 copies at 19c each in the school shop.
    How much did she pay altogether? _____ S18

19. 6 ÷ 2 = ___ S19

20. 5)75 S20

21. 8 ÷ 3 = _____ S21

22. 7)67 S22

1

23. Mr O'Reilly goes swimming every day in the local pool. If he swims 84 lengths of the pool in a full week, how many lengths does he swim every day? _____ S23

24.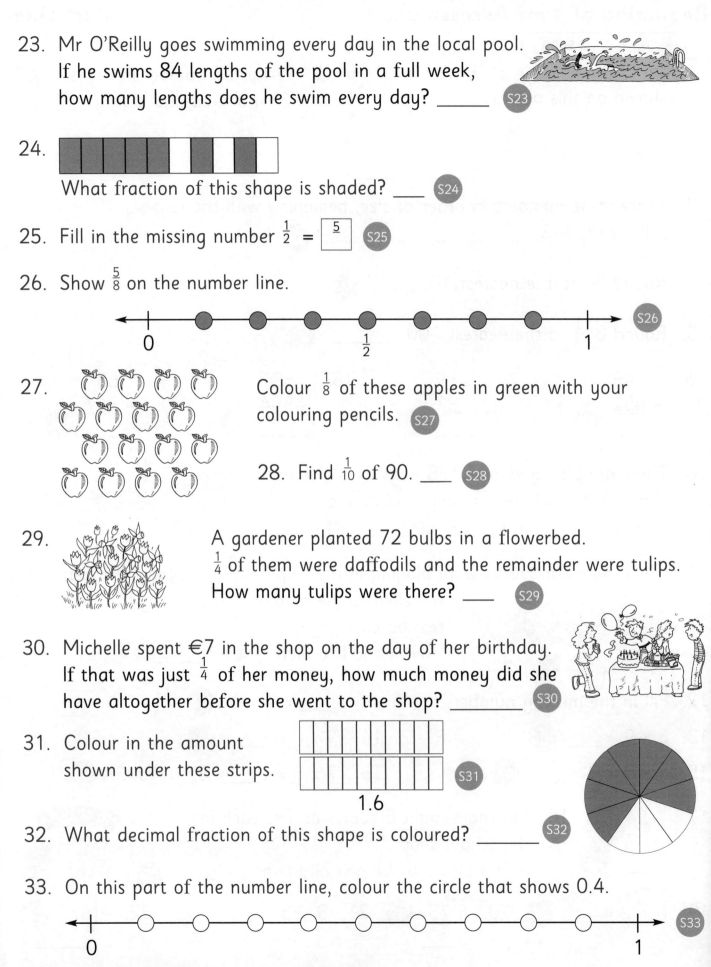

What fraction of this shape is shaded? ___ S24

25. Fill in the missing number $\frac{1}{2}$ = $\boxed{\dfrac{5}{}}$ S25

26. Show $\frac{5}{8}$ on the number line.

0    $\frac{1}{2}$ 1   S26

27. Colour $\frac{1}{8}$ of these apples in green with your colouring pencils. S27

28. Find $\frac{1}{10}$ of 90. ___ S28

29. A gardener planted 72 bulbs in a flowerbed. $\frac{1}{4}$ of them were daffodils and the remainder were tulips. How many tulips were there? ___ S29

30. Michelle spent €7 in the shop on the day of her birthday. If that was just $\frac{1}{4}$ of her money, how much money did she have altogether before she went to the shop? _____ S30

31. Colour in the amount shown under these strips.

1.6   S31

32. What decimal fraction of this shape is coloured? _____ S32

33. On this part of the number line, colour the circle that shows 0.4.

0   1   S33

2

34.  This school has 10 classrooms. 3 of the classrooms are empty at the moment. **What decimal fraction of the classrooms is empty?** _____ S34

35. Fill in the missing number in this pattern: 36, 30, 24, ___ 12, 6 S35

36. Find the next number in this pattern: 2, 7, 12, 17, 22, ___ S36

37. Find the missing number in the box: 16 + ☐ = 24 S37

38. Write a word story to match this number sentence: 6 + ☐ = 18 S38

_____

_____

39. Write a word story to match this number sentence: 24 − ☐ = 8 S39

_____

_____

40. Look at these 3 shapes and colour the hexagon. S40

41. Colour the shape that has 4 equal sides. S41

42. Tick the name of this shape in the list. S42

43. How many edges are on a cuboid? ___ S43

44. Name the shape that has 4 triangular faces and 1 square face. **Choose from this list.** _____ S44

Part One: Skills mastered ☐ 44

3

45. Put a tick in the box beside the letter that is symmetrical.

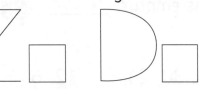

46. Draw the axis of symmetry in this letter.

47. Tick the box that is beside a line that is vertical.

(a)  (b) 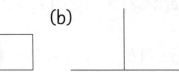 (c)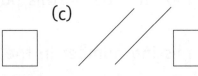

48. Which of the lines (1, 2, 3, 4 or 5) is horizontal? ____

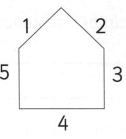

49. Use arrows to mark the parallel lines in this shape.

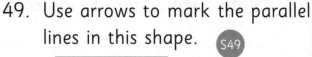

50. Which of these angles is greater than a right angle? ____

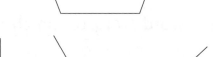
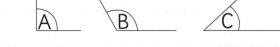

51. Is this line (a) 7cm, (b) 8cm, or (c) 5cm in length? ____ cm

52. 156cm = ____ m _____ cm

53.

m	cm
3	58
+ 2	74

54.

m	cm
5	32
− 1	67

55. The Murphys' car is 3m 96cm long. The O'Neills' car is 85cm longer. How long is the O'Neills' car? _____

56. Niamh is 1m 62cm in height. Her little brother is 70cm less than that. How tall is her brother? _____

57.

kg	g
1	450
+ 3	865

58.

kg	g
7	132
− 3	485

59. Michael is carrying an 800g sliced pan and a 500g jar of honey in the bag. What is the total weight of these items in kg and g? ____ kg _____ g

60. By how much is one bag lighter than the other? _____ S60

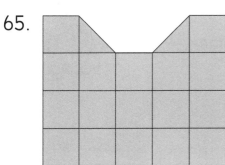

1kg 300g   2kg 750g

61.

l	ml
3	675
+ 2	850

_____ S61

62.

l	ml
6	895
− 3	968

_____ S62

63. There were $6\frac{1}{4}$ litres of petrol in a lawnmower and Mrs Brennan put in another 2l 750ml. How much petrol altogether was in the lawnmower then?
____l _____ml S63

64. There were $9\frac{1}{2}$ litres of oil in a container. 2l 750ml of it was used. How much oil was left in the container? ____l _____ml S64

9.5 Litres

65.

What is the area of this shape?
_____ square units S65

66. What time is shown on this clock face?
___ minutes past _____ S66

67. Write the time shown here.
___ minutes to ___ S67

9:55

68. Michelle ate her dinner at twenty to seven. Show this time on the clock face. S68

69. Write in the numbers on this watch face to show twenty to eight. S69

70.

This bus was due to come at 4:56 but it didn't arrive until 5:03.
How many minutes late was it? ___ minutes S70

71. 110 minutes = ___ hour ____ minutes S71

72. 2 hours 36 minutes = ____ minutes S72

73. How many minutes does it take the train to go from Hightown to Lowtown? _____ S73

Train Timetable	
Bigtown	9:36
Smalltown	10:12
Hightown	10:56
Lowtown	11:28

74. Lisa is going on her holidays on 19 August. **What day is that?**

_____

75. 8 weeks = ___ days

76. €3.94 = ___ c

77. 209c = € ___

78. €3.87 + €2.59 = ___

79. €12.72 – €3.98 = ___

80. Joseph bought a magazine for €2.98 and a drink for €1.39. How much did he pay altogether for the 2 items? _____

81. Joseph handed in €5 for the drink and the magazine. How much change should he get? _____

82.

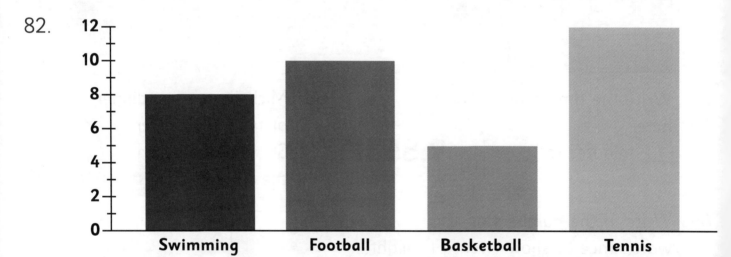

This bar chart shows the favourite sports of a group of children.

How many children were in the group? ___

83. Put a tick (✔) in the box beside the word that best describes the sentence below.
'Next year there will be school on Saturdays.'

| likely | ☐ | unlikely | ☐ | S83 |

Part Two: Skills mastered ⟋ 39

Total number of skills mastered (Part One and Part Two) ⟋ 83

th	h	t	u

1. Show this number on the abacus picture.
   Three thousand two hundred and nine (S1)

2. Write down the number: **three thousand seven hundred and ninety-six**. _____ (S2)

3. Put these numbers in order, beginning with the smallest.
   4796, 4769, 4697, 4679. _____, _____, _____, _____ (S3)

4. Round 3659 to the nearest thousand. _____ (S4)

5. 3246 + 1543 = _____ (S5)

6. 2867 + 965 = _____ (S6)

7.   6789
   − 1274
   _____ (S7)

8. 9201 − 896 = _____ (S8)

9. 2968 men and 4867 women attended an outdoor concert in Dublin last summer. How many people altogether attended the concert? _____ (S9)

10. Patrick Street library has 8631 books in the fiction section. 4739 of them are out on loan.
    How many are still on the shelves? _____ (S10)

11. 8 + 8 + 8 + 8 + 8 = ____ x 8 (S11)

12.   26
    x 8
    ____ (S12)

13.   468
    x 7
    ____ (S14)

14. 5 x 9 = ____ x 5 (S17)

7

15. $9 \times 8 = (6 \times 8) + (\underline{} \times 8)$

16. If a box can hold 148 oranges, how many oranges would fit in 6 boxes? _____ S20

17. $378 \div 7 =$ ____ S21   18. $315 \div 4 =$ ____ S22

19. 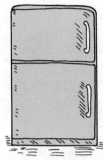 This fridge costs 6 times as much as the electric kettle. If the fridge is priced at €474, find the cost of the kettle. _____ S23

20. Colour $\frac{2}{5}$ of this rectangle.

21. $\frac{2}{3} = \boxed{\dfrac{}{9}}$ S25

22. Put these fractions in order, beginning with the smallest.

$\frac{2}{5}$, $\frac{7}{10}$, $\frac{1}{2}$ ☐ ☐ ☐ S26

23. Write the missing fraction on this part of the number line. S27

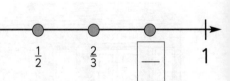

$0 \qquad \frac{1}{6} \qquad \frac{1}{3} \qquad \frac{1}{2} \qquad \frac{2}{3} \qquad \boxed{} \qquad 1$

24. Find $\frac{1}{5}$ of €280. _____ S28

25. Find the missing number. ____ is $\frac{1}{4}$ of 28 S29

26. John has €15 in the bank. That is $\frac{3}{5}$ of his money. How much money has he got altogether? _____ S30

8

27. Máire got €30 from her aunt for her birthday. She spent $\frac{5}{6}$ of it on a jumper. **How much did she pay for the jumper?** _____ S31

28. Choose the word that best describes this sentence. 'It will rain next week.'

    | likely |, | certainly | or | impossible | _____ S98

29. **Noel is running late for school this morning because his alarm didn't go off. He forgot to get a note from his parents to say why he is late.**

    Now look at the sentences below. Rewrite them in the order that Noel is likely to deal with the problem. Start with the most likely.

    - Noel will turn back and get a note from his parents.
    - He will tell the teacher that he met a lion on the way to school and couldn't get by until it left.
    - He will explain to the teacher that he overslept.
    - He will say that his dog was sick and he had to look after it for a while.

    S99

    (a) _____

    (b) _____

    (c) _____

    (d) _____

Skills mastered ⎗29

9

1. 389 + 4063 = _____ S6

2. 8120 – 4896 = _____ S8

3. This restaurant served 1096 meals in December and 978 meals in January. How many meals is that altogether? _____ S9

4. The population of Newtown is 3076 and the population of Oldtown is 1809. How many more people live in Newtown than in Oldtown? _____ S10

5. 37 x 56 = _____ S13

6. 8 x 509 = _____ S14

7. 53 x 176 = _____ S15

8. 0 x 245 = _____ S16

9. (3 x 8) x 7 = 3 x (___ x 7) S19

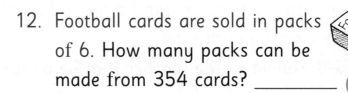

10. Last August a newsagent ordered 40 packets of copies. Each packet contained 32 copies. How many copies did he order? _____ S20

11. 399 ÷ 5 = _____ S22

12. Football cards are sold in packs of 6. How many packs can be made from 354 cards? _____ S23

13. Colour $\frac{5}{12}$ of these counters. S24

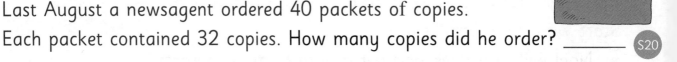

14. $\frac{1}{5}$ of 125 = ___ S28

15. Rewrite these numbers in order, starting with the smallest. 0.9, 0.95, 9.05, 0.59 _____ S32

16. Write $\frac{6}{10}$ as a decimal. _____ S33

17. $5\frac{9}{100}$ = 5._____ S34

18. Write 136.78 in expanded form. _____ + _____ + _____ + _____ + _____ S35

19. Fill in the missing number on this part of the number line.

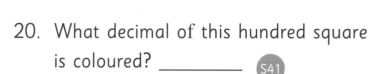
4.1   4.11   4.12   4.13   4.14   4.15   4.16   4.17   4.18   4.19   ☐

20. What decimal of this hundred square is coloured? _____ S41

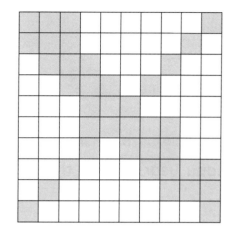

21. Continue this number pattern: 2983, 2984, 2986, 2989, _____ S42

22. Fill in the missing word to describe this triangle.
This is an _____ triangle. S49

23. Fill in the missing word.
An octagon has _____ angles. S50

24. Rewrite 509c using the euro symbol and the decimal point. _____ S92

25. €8.72 = _____c S93

26. Ms Green, the principal of Scoil Treasa, bought 4 of these CD players for the school.
How much did they cost altogether? _____ S94

€89.50

27. How much change would you get out of €10 if you bought 6 oranges at 69c each? _____ S95

Skills mastered ☐/27

11

1. 768 + 5954 = _____ S6

2. 5102 – 3708 = _____ S8

3. Find the total cost of a computer, a printer and a computer desk._____ S9

4. Scoil Bhríde was built in 1963. How many years ago is that? _____ S10

5. 24 x 307 = _____ S15

6.  This cash box contains 125 five euro notes and 263 ten euro notes. How much money is in the cash box? _____ S20

7. 546 ÷ 7 = _____ S21

8. Cakes are packed in boxes of 8. How many boxes are needed to pack 192 cakes? _____ S23

9. What fraction of these pencils is coloured? ⬚— S24

10. $\frac{6}{9}$ = $\frac{2}{\boxed{}}$ S25

11. Rewrite these fractions in order, starting with the largest.

$\frac{1}{9}$, $\frac{1}{4}$, $\frac{1}{3}$, $\frac{9}{10}$, $\frac{1}{5}$ _____ S26

12. Put $\frac{3}{5}$ in the correct place on this part of the number line. S27

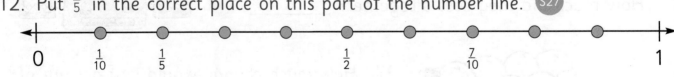

0    $\frac{1}{10}$ $\frac{1}{5}$ $\frac{1}{2}$ $\frac{7}{10}$ 1

13. $\frac{1}{8}$ of 704 = _____ S28

14. 18 is $\frac{\boxed{}}{\boxed{}}$ of 54. S29

15. $\frac{5}{9}$ of a number is 55. What is the number? _____ S30

16. Patricia read $\frac{1}{5}$ of her book in 1 evening.

    If she read 26 pages, how many pages were in the book? _____

17. 27.06 + 38.95 = _____   18. 96.01 − 49.75 = _____

19. 8 x 9.67 = _____   20. 90.78 ÷ 3 = _____

21. By how much is (27.32 − 9.75) less than (53.25 ÷ 3)? _____ S41

22. Name this shape.  S51

    _____

23. Fill in the missing letter.

    Line ___ is perpendicular to the coloured line. S54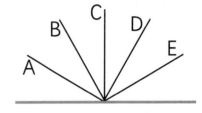

24. Which letter in the word BOX has intersecting lines? _____ S55

25. 6kg 296g + 3kg 54g = ____kg ____g S70

26. 10kg 15g − 3kg 250g = ____kg ____g S71

27. Jack bought 454g of butter, 350g
    of tomatoes and a pizza that
    weighed 376g. What was the total
    weight of the 3 items? _____ S74

Skills mastered ╱27

1. 1508 + 3647 = _____ S6

2. 7024 − 3675 = _____ S8

3.  A gardener planted 965 tulip bulbs and 750 daffodil bulbs in St Stephen's Green. How many bulbs did he plant altogether? _____ S9

4. Siobhán had €825 in the bank. She took out €450 to pay for a holiday. How much money had she left in her account? _____ S10

5. 36 x 79 = _____ S13

6. All of the 145 children in Third and Fourth Class in Scoil Eoin bought a Maths book costing €12. How much money did they spend on Maths books altogether? _____ S20

7. 864 ÷ 6 = _____ S21

8.  Mr Hanley divided a box of 98 sweets equally among the 7 children in his Fourth Class at a Christmas party. How many sweets did each child receive? _____ S23

9. $\frac{1}{6}$ of 132 = _____ S28

10. 16.8 + 37.59 = _____ S37

11. 28 + ☐ = 97 S43

Write a word problem in your copy for each of the 4 number sentences below and find the answers.

12. 24 + 38 = ☐ S44

13. 81 − ☐ = 25 S45

14. 9 x ☐ = 234 S46

15. 368 ÷ 16 = ☐ S47

16. Write a number sentence for this word problem and find the answer.

A box of oranges contains 84 oranges. How many oranges would 8 boxes contain?

_____ S48

17. 639cm = _____m _____cm S57

18. 2860m = _____._____km S58

19. 327cm = ___ ⬜ m S59

20. Measure the perimeter of this shape. _____cm S60

21. 8km 75m + 13km 390m = _____km _____m S61

22. 12m 25cm – 7m 97cm = _____m _____cm S62

23. 9 x 5km 265m = _____ S63

24. 3 |29m 61cm S64

   _____

25. A carpenter cut a plank of wood measuring 1m 52cm into 4 equal lengths. How long was each piece of wood? _____ S65

26. 3209ml = ___.___l S76

27. 7l 509ml + 3l 762ml = _____ S78

28. 12l 275ml – 8l 488ml = _____ S79

29. Write the correct time under this clock. S83

___ minutes ___ ___ o'clock

30. How many minutes until 8 o'clock?

 S84

_____ minutes

15

31. Draw in the hands on this clock to show the correct time. S85

$2:25$ =

32. 146 minutes = ___ hrs ___ mins S86

33. 52 days = __ weeks __ days S87

34. Read this section of a bus timetable and fill in the missing numbers. **The longest journey lasted __ hours __ minutes.** S88

Depart		Arrive	
Dublin	8:30	Portlaoise	10:15
Dublin	9:05	Limerick	12:40
Dublin	10:15	Arklow	12:50

35.

September						
M	**T**	**W**	**T**	**F**	**S**	**S**
	1	2	3	4	5	6
7	8	9	10	11	12	13
14	15	16	17	18	19	20
21	22	23	24	25	26	27
28	29	30				

Look at this calendar page and then answer the question.
What date is the third Thursday in September? _____ S89

36. Marie and Ciarán will both be 10 years old this year. Ciarán's birthday is 29 August and Marie's birthday is 12 September. How many days older than Marie is Ciarán? _____ S90

37. Stephen is studying for his Junior Cert. He spent 2 hours 50 minutes studying on Monday and 3 hours 20 minutes studying on Tuesday. How many hours and minutes is that altogether? ___hours ___minutes S91

38. Aideen had €12.34 and she spent €5.79 on a present for her dad. How much money had she left? _____ S94

39. Brian had €4.30 and his mother gave him €5. He then gave $\frac{1}{3}$ of his money to his sister Kate. How much money did he give to Kate? _____ S95

Skills mastered / 39

Fourth Class

1. Draw the vertical axis of symmetry in this hexagon. S52

2. Draw in the missing half of this shape to make it symmetrical. S53

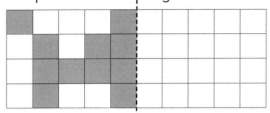

3. Use these words to name each angle correctly: acute, right, obtuse.

_____   _____   _____ S56

4. 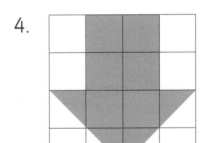 Find the area of this shape by counting the cm². _____ cm² S66

5. $3\frac{1}{2}$ kg = _____ g   S67

6. 5090g = ___._____ kg   S68

7. 2kg 250g = ___ kg   S69

8. 6 x 3kg 312g = ___kg _____g   S72

9. 7kg 208g ÷ 4 = _____   S73

10. 3l 500ml = _____ ml   S75

11. 5l 750ml = ___ l   S77

12. 5 x 3l 485ml = _____   S80

13. 14l 142ml ÷ 6 = _____   S81

 14. How much milk would be left in a 2l carton of milk if you poured 350ml of milk into each of these 4 glasses? _____ S82

15. This line graph shows the number of new cars sold by a garage over 3 months.
How many cars were sold altogether in the 3 months? _____ **S96**

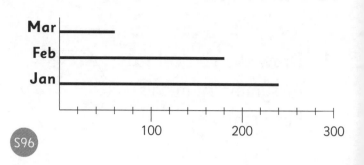

16.

A group of 69 people was asked which sport they preferred, hurling or Gaelic football. This pie chart shows the result. $\frac{1}{3}$ of the group said they preferred hurling. How many people preferred Gaelic football? _____ **S97**

Skills mastered /16

Multiplication

1. 9 x 2 = ___	11. 8 x 10 = ___	21. 9 x 7 = ___	31. 10 x 5 = ___
2. 7 x 3 = ___	12. 5 x 2 = ___	22. 10 x 10 = ___	32. 9 x 6 = ___
3. 6 x 4 = ___	13. 4 x 3 = ___	23. 6 x 2 = ___	33. 5 x 3 = ___
4. 5 x 5 = ___	14. 7 x 6 = ___	24. 8 x 3 = ___	34. 9 x 9 = ___
5. 4 x 2 = ___	15. 8 x 8 = ___	25. 10 x 4 = ___	35. 7 x 2 = ___
6. 6 x 6 = ___	16. 1 x 9 = ___	26. 6 x 5 = ___	36. 5 x 4 = ___
7. 10 x 3 = ___	17. 8 x 4 = ___	27. 8 x 6 = ___	37. 7 x 5 = ___
8. 9 x 4 = ___	18. 6 x 3 = ___	28. 9 x 5 = ___	38. 9 x 3 = ___
9. 8 x 5 = ___	19. 8 x 2 = ___	29. 7 x 7 = ___	39. 10 x 6 = ___
10. 0 x 9 = ___	20. 7 x 8 = ___	30. 7 x 4 = ___	40. 9 x 8 = ___

Total number of multiplication facts mastered: ____

Division

1. 18 ÷ 9 = ___	11. 80 ÷ 8 = ___	21. 63 ÷ 9 = ___	31. 50 ÷ 10 = ___
2. 21 ÷ 7 = ___	12. 10 ÷ 5 = ___	22. 100 ÷ 10 = ___	32. 54 ÷ 9 = ___
3. 24 ÷ 6 = ___	13. 12 ÷ 4 = ___	23. 12 ÷ 6 = ___	33. 15 ÷ 5 = ___
4. 25 ÷ 5 = ___	14. 42 ÷ 7 = ___	24. 24 ÷ 8 = ___	34. 81 ÷ 9 = ___
5. 8 ÷ 4 = ___	15. 64 ÷ 8 = ___	25. 40 ÷ 10 = ___	35. 14 ÷ 7 = ___
6. 36 ÷ 6 = ___	16. 9 ÷ 9 = ___	26. 30 ÷ 6 = ___	36. 20 ÷ 5 = ___
7. 70 ÷ 10 = ___	17. 32 ÷ 8 = ___	27. 48 ÷ 8 = ___	37. 35 ÷ 7 = ___
8. 36 ÷ 9 = ___	18. 18 ÷ 6 = ___	28. 45 ÷ 9 = ___	38. 27 ÷ 9 = ___
9. 40 ÷ 8 = ___	19. 16 ÷ 8 = ___	29. 49 ÷ 7 = ___	39. 60 ÷ 10 = ___
10. 0 ÷ 9 = ___	20. 56 ÷ 7 = ___	30. 28 ÷ 7 = ___	40. 72 ÷ 9 = ___

Total number of division facts mastered: ____

Fourth Class End of Year Assessment*   **Part One**

1. Write the value of the underlined digit. 9<u>1</u>64. _____

2. Write the number shown on this abacus picture.

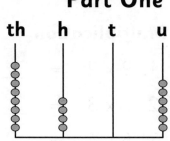

th	h	t	u

_____

3. Write these numbers in order, starting with the biggest.
7095, 7905, 7950, 7059, 7509 _____, _____, _____, _____, _____

4. Round 5429 to the nearest thousand. _____

5. 493 + 1506 = _____   6. 2635 + 1768 = _____

7. 5768 – 1546 = _____   8. 6305 – 2757 = _____

9. A music store had 3286 CDs in stock before a delivery of 4540 new CDs arrived.
How many CDs were in the store after the delivery? _____

10. By how much is 7206 greater than 5639? _____

11. 7 + 7 + 7 + 7 + 7 + 7 = __ x 7   12. 7 x 36 = _____

13. 28 x 45 = _____   14. 5 x 247 = _____   15. 35 x 164 = _____

16. 0 x 70 = _____   17. 2 x 9 = 9 x __ = __   18. 9 x 7 = (3 x 7) + (__ x 7)

19. (6 x 5) x 4 = __ x (__ x 4)

20. Jason saved €45 every week for 9 weeks.
How much money did he save altogether? _____

21. 291 ÷ 3 = _____   22. 478 ÷ 6 = _____

23. St John's School receives the same number of cartons of milk every day.
If 625 cartons were delivered in one school week, how many cartons were delivered each day? _____

---

*   Note to teacher: The questions in this assessment match the Fourth Class skills 1-99, i.e. Question 1 tests Skill 1, Question 2 tests Skill 2 and so on.

24. What fraction of this shape is coloured? 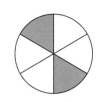

25. $\frac{5}{6} = \frac{\boxed{}}{12}$

26. Write these fractions in order, starting with the smallest

$\frac{1}{5}, \quad \frac{1}{2}, \quad \frac{3}{4}, \quad \frac{11}{12}, \quad \frac{1}{3}$ _____

27. Put $\frac{2}{3}$ in the correct place on this part of the number line.

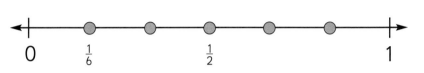

28. $\frac{1}{9}$ of 72 = ____   29. 25 is $\boxed{\frac{}{}}$ of 100   30. $\frac{3}{5}$ of a number is 99. What is the number? ____

31. Annette spent 68c on an ice cream and she had $\frac{3}{4}$ of her money left. How much money had she to start with? _____

32. Circle the larger number: 29.37 or 29.73.

33. What decimal of this shape is coloured? 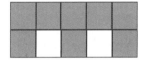 _____

34. Write $\frac{7}{100}$ as a decimal. ____   35. Write 87.54 in expanded form. ___ + ___ + ___ + ___

36. Fill in the missing decimal on this part of the number line.

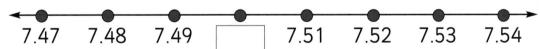

7.47   7.48   7.49   ☐   7.51   7.52   7.53   7.54

37.   16.87
    + 14.96
    _____

38. 61.28
   − 29.59
   _____

39. 47.34
   x   6
   _____

40. 3 ⟌ 79.02
    _____

41. How much would each child get if €73 was divided equally among 4 children? _____

Part One: Skills mastered ◹41

21

42. Continue this number pattern: 4023, 4014, 4005, _____

43. 9 x ☐ = 306

In your copy, write a word problem to match these number sentences and find the missing numbers.

44. 13 + ☐ = 37   45. 125 – 36 = ☐   46. 8 x 25 = ☐   47. 126 ÷ ☐ = 9

48. Write a number sentence to match this word problem.
64 children were divided into groups of 8 for a Maths activity. How many children were in each group? _____

49. Name this shape. _____   50. A rhombus has _____ pairs of parallel lines.

51. Name this shape. _____

52. Draw the horizontal line of symmetry in this square.

53. Draw the missing half of this shape to make it symmetrical.

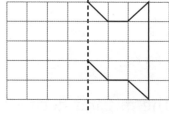

54. Fill in the missing letters.
Line ___ is perpendicular to line ___.

55. Draw a line that intersects line A.

56. Shade the obtuse angle. (a)   (b)   (c)

57. 3000m = ____ km   58. 275cm = ___.___m   59. 4350 m = ___ ☐—km

60. Measure the length of the perimeter of this rhombus. _____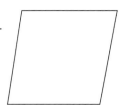

61.
m cm
  6 73
+ 3 59
_____

62.
km   m
  7 250
− 4 395
_____

63.
m cm
  6 26
x   7
_____

64. 8 ⎷18km 800m
_____

65. Ms King's car is 3m 37cm long. Her garage is 5m 10cm long. How much longer than the car is the garage? _____

66. Find the area of this shape by counting the cm². _____

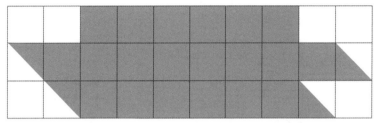

67. 3245g = ___kg ___g
68. 4197g = ___.___kg
69. 2569g = __ ⬚/⬚ kg

70.
kg   g
  3 296
+ 2 875
_____

71.
kg   g
  8 125
− 5 675
_____

72. 4kg 370g
x   8
_____

73. 7 ⎷9kg 163g
_____

74. Find the weight of 5 bags of potatoes if 1 bag weighs 3kg 400g. _____

75. 2065 ml = ___l ___ml
76. 4385ml = ___.___l
77. 6l 750ml = ___ ⬚/⬚ l

78.
l ml
  5 975
+ 2 386
_____

79.
l ml
  8 375
− 5 879
_____

80.
l ml
  5 395
x   6
_____

81. 8 ⎷27l 608ml
_____

82. The total capacity of these 4 cartons is 1ℓ 680mℓ. What is the capacity of each carton? _____

83. Draw hands on this clock to show 22 minutes past 7.

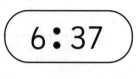

84. How many minutes until 7 o'clock?

6 : 37

_____ minutes

85. Write in the correct time on this digital clock.

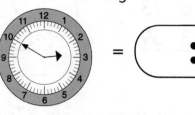 = ⬭ :

86. 2 hours 45 minutes = _____ minutes

87. 6 weeks = _____ days

88. This is part of a TV timetable.

9:05	Comedy Time
9:40	News
10:05	Sports Scene
11:00	Music Show
11:45	Closedown

Fill in the missing number of minutes.
Sports Scene lasts _____ minutes longer than the news.

89. Fill in the missing day.
21 June is on a _____.

| June | | | | | | |
M	T	W	T	F	S	S
				1	2	3
4	5	6	7	8	9	10
11	12	13	14	15	16	17
18	19	20	21	22	23	24
25	26	27	28	29	30	

90.

The Ryan family went on holidays on 3 June and returned on 14 June. How many nights were they away from home? _____

91. Martina Rooney usually works 6 hours 30 minutes a day in a factory. She left work 2 hours 45 minutes early last Friday. How many hours and minutes did she work on that day? _____ hours _____ minutes

92. Write 476c using the euro symbol and the decimal point. _____

93. €5.28 = _____c

94. A teacher spent €27 buying 6 copies of a book.
    How much did each book cost? _____

95. Seán bought a magazine for €2.47 and a sandwich for €2.75.
    How much change did he get out of a 20 euro note? _____

96. This line graph shows the number of people who attended a pantomime in a
    Cork theatre over one weekend.
    How many more people
    attended the pantomime on
    Friday than on Sunday? _____

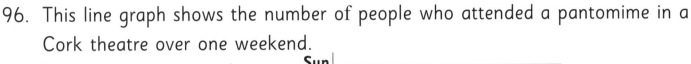

97. 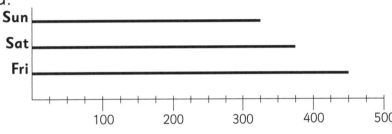 This pie chart shows the favourite pastimes of 76 children.
    How many more children preferred sports to watching
    television? _____

98. Choose the most suitable word from the list to go with the sentence below.
    'All of the Fourth Class children in St Peter's School have at least 4 sisters.'
    | likely |, | definitely | or | unlikely | _____

99. Look at this picture and then number these sentences 1, 2 and 3 in the
    order you think they are most likely to occur.

    ☐ The sun will shine soon.

    ☐ The children will rush into their houses.

    ☐ The children will splash in the puddle.

    Part Two: Skills mastered ⧄58

    Total number of skills mastered
    (Part One and Part Two) ⧄99

25

Third Class Skills Record Sheet

Pupil's name: _____

Strand: Number

Place value: | 1 | 2 | 3 | 4 | 5 |

Addition and subtraction: | 6 | 7 | 8 | 9 | 10 | 11 |

Multiplication: | 12 | 13 | 14 | 15 | 16 | 17 | 18 |

Division: | 19 | 20 | 21 | 22 | 23 |

Fractions: | 24 | 25 | 26 | 27 | 28 | 29 | 30 |

Decimals: | 31 | 32 | 33 | 34 |

See the Third Class Skills List in MM4 Solutions Book to cross-reference the skill numbers listed here.

Strand: Algebra

Number patterns and sequences: | 35 | 36 |

Number sentences: | 37 | 38 | 39 |

Strand: Shape and space

2-D shapes: | 40 | 41 |

3-D shapes: | 42 | 43 | 44 |

Symmetry: | 45 | 46 |

Lines and angles: | 47 | 48 | 49 | 50 |

Strand: Measures

Length: | 51 | 52 | 53 | 54 | 55 | 56 |

Weight: | 57 | 58 | 59 | 60 |

Capacity: | 61 | 62 | 63 | 64 |

Area: | 65 |

Time: | 66 | 67 | 68 | 69 | 70 | 71 | 72 | 73 | 74 | 75 |

Money: | 76 | 77 | 78 | 79 | 80 | 81 |

Strand: Data

Representing and interpreting data: | 82 |

Chance: | 83 |

Skills mastered / 83

Fourth Class Skills Record Sheet

Pupil's name: _____

Strand: Number

Place value: | 1 | | 2 | | 3 | | 4 |

Addition and subtraction: | 5 | | 6 | | | | 7 | | 8 | | | |

| 9 | | | | | 10 | | | |

Multiplication: | 11 | | 12 | | 13 | | 14 | | | 15 | | | 16 | | 17 | | 18 | |

| 19 | | 20 | | | |

Division: | 21 | | | 22 | | 23 | | | |

Fractions: | 24 | | | 25 | | 26 | | 27 | | |

| 28 | | | | 29 | | | 30 | | 31 | | |

Decimals: | 32 | | 33 | | 34 | | 35 | | 36 | | 37 | | 38 | | 39 | | 40 | |

| 41 | | |

See the Fourth Class Skills List in MM4 Solutions Book to cross-reference the skill numbers listed here.

Strand: Algebra

Patterns: | 42 | | Number sentences: | 43 | | 44 | | 45 | | 46 | | 47 | | 48 | |

Strand: Shape and space

2-D shapes: | 49 | | 50 | | 3-D shapes: | 51 | | Symmetry: | 52 | | 53 | |

Lines and angles: | 54 | | 55 | | 56 | |

Strand: Measures

Length: | 57 | | 58 | | 59 | | 60 | | 61 | | 62 | | 63 | | 64 | | 65 | |

Area: | 66 | |

Weight: | 67 | | 68 | | 69 | | 70 | | 71 | | 72 | | 73 | | 74 | |

Capacity: | 75 | | 76 | | 77 | | 78 | | 79 | | 80 | | 81 | | 82 | |

Time: | 83 | | 84 | | 85 | | 86 | | 87 | | 88 | | 89 | | 90 | | 91 | |

Money: | 92 | | 93 | | 94 | | 95 | | |

Strand: Data

Data: | 96 | | 97 | | Chance: | 98 | | 99 | |

Skills mastered ⟋99

28